Public Lives
Private Prayers

Public Lives
Private Prayers

Bill Bradley *Joan Baez* Ann Landers *art linkletter* Ed McMahon Matthew McConaughey
George Bush **Victor Borge** **Seamus Heaney** Tim Russert *Mickey Spillane* **Brigitte Bardot**
Mario Cuomo *Fr. Theodore Hesburgh* jerry lewis **Yogi Berra** *Danielle Steel* **Queen Noor**
Rev. Desmond Tutu *Dale Evans Rogers* Margaret Thatcher Lauren Hutton *and more. . .*

Mary Reath

SORIN BOOKS   Notre Dame, IN

A c k n o w l e d g m e n t s

The publisher and author gratefully acknowledge permission to reprint the following:

Frost, Robert. "Stopping by Woods on a Snowy Evening," New Hampshire, 1923, Holt, NY.

"My Prayer," copyright Yehudi Menuhin. Used with permission by the Estate of Yehudi Menuhin. All rights reserved.

Every effort has been made to give proper acknowledgment to authors and copyright holders of the texts herein. If any omissions or errors have been made, please notify the publisher who will correct it in future editions.

Except as noted on p. 127, scripture quotations are from the *New Revised Standard Version* of the Bible, copyright © 1993 and 1989 by the Division of Christian Education of the National Council of Churches of Christ in the U.S.A. Used by permission. All rights reserved.

International Standard Book Number: 1-893732-26-6
Cover and text design by Brian C. Conley
Printed and bound in the United States of America.

Library of Congress Cataloging-in-Publication Data
Public lives, private prayers / [compiled by] Mary Reath.
    p. cm.
  ISBN 1-893732-26-6 (pbk.)
1. Spiritual life--Quotations, maxims, etc. 2.
Celebrities--Quotations. I. Reath, Mary.
BL624 .P83 2000
291.4'33--dc21
                                00-011333

I offer a sincere thank you to all who took my request for a favorite prayer seriously, and to all who have helped me to think about and develop this book. As I received the responses, I gradually came to believe that these collected writings, especially given their connection to real people, might have transforming powers.

For Henry and Frances

Contents

Introduction

So you pray to learn how to pray.
—Thomas Merton (1915-1968)

This anthology of prayers and poems presents the spiritual and religious voices of some very public people. By sharing these prayers, they have opened themselves up to a community of readers, and generously contributed to the evocation of the spiritual life. To hear them speak in this range of voices is revealing, and what they have chosen is accessible and sometimes profound. Their choices and their words might surprise us if we forget that life has shaped these contributors in strong ways.

It does not seem that we can get to faith logically, nor can we command its existence. It has to be personal, and it needs to be awakened or evoked. Then, it needs to be nurtured. These prayers and poems have the power to awaken and develop this sense of the sacred. Many of the selections do just that by highlighting quotations and poems that are at times not very well known, at times not even recognized as being prayerful.

I hope that this collection will be an instrument for enlivening your religious and spiritual life, in its private and its public senses. Sometimes, something in our deepest being is expressed when we pray or experiment with praying. These prayers express many of our images of God—or something Other—and some of our yearnings and fears, our doubts, our praises, and our petitions. They can help us to transform our feelings into faith. They can be quite poetic, emotional, or intellectual, but, in a scientific age, they are entirely non rational. To pray calls for both free will and submission.

I hope that as you read this book, you will find something that you are looking for. Better yet, I pray that you will find something that surprises you, that you didn't even know you were looking for, something that pierces your heart and excites your sense of the *wholly other.*

And now let's tune our instruments.
—George Herbert (1593-1633)

chapter one

Living

Bill Bradley
Former Basketball Star and U.S. Senator

I have enclosed a Buddhist text that I feel best describes my lifestyle and ambitions. The words on the card reflect my ideas about the union of work and play. From my college basketball and Knick days to my terms in the Senate, I have tried to strive for excellence. It's easy to strive for excellence when you enjoy what you do and I have been blessed in my life choices.

The Master in the art of living
makes little distinction between
his work and his play,
his labor and his leisure,
his mind and his body,
his education and his recreation,
his love and his religion.
He hardly knows which is which.
He simply pursues his vision of excellence
in whatever he does,
leaving others to decide
whether he is working or playing.
To him he is always doing both.

—Zen Buddhist Text

Matthew McConaughey
Actor

McConaughey offered the same Zen Buddhist text as Bradley, with the following explanation: *Here's one that helps me see the big picture and keeps me from polarizing. It really adds a little "rock 'n roll" to the responsibility for me. Naomi Judd passed this on to me a couple of years ago. It's also one definition in my favorite perspective: j.k.livin (just keep living).*

Madeleine L'Engle
Author of A Wrinkle in Time

Listen to the exhortation of the dawn.
Look to this day, for it is life, the very life of life.
In its brief course lie all the verities and realities of our existence.
The glory of action, the bliss of growth, the splendor of beauty.
For yesterday is but a dream, and tomorrow only a vision.
But today well lived makes every yesterday a dream of happiness,
And every tomorrow a vision of hope.
Look well therefore to this day. Such is the salutation of the dawn.

— *Kalidasa, Indian Dramatist*

Elaine Pagels
Author and Professor of Religion

Here's a saying from the Gospel of Thomas:

Jesus said, "If you bring forth what is in you,
what you bring forth will save you.
If you do not bring forth what is in you,
what you do not bring forth will destroy you."

Elizabeth Gilchrist
Author

Take short views, hope for the best, and trust in God.

—Sydney Smith (1771–1845)

Huston Smith
Author of The World's Religions

from "Orion"

The choice is always ours. Then, let me choose
The longest art, the hard Promethean way
Cherishingly to tend and feed and fan
That inward fire, whose small precarious flame,
Kindled or quenched, creates
The noble or the ignoble men we are,
The worlds we live in and the very fates,
Our bright or muddy star.

—Aldous Huxley (1894–1963)

[Handwritten annotations:]

Santa Barbara, CA 93109

Sept. 1, 1998

Dear Mr. [illegible],

Thank you for including me in your inquiries. I do, indeed, have a favorite spiritual quotation:

"Take short views, hope for the best, and trust in God."

Sydney Smith
1771 – 1845

Please let me know when your [illegible]

All best wishes,

Sincerely,
Elizabeth Gilchrist

Theodosius

M e t r o p o l i t a n   o f   A l l   A m e r i c a   a n d   C a n a d a
a n d   P r i m a t e , O r t h o d o x   C h u r c h   i n   A m e r i c a

This prayer is a favorite of many Orthodox Christians.

Prayer at the Beginning of the Day

O Lord, grant me to greet the coming day in peace. Help me in all things to rely upon thy holy will. In every hour of the day reveal thy will to me. Bless my dealings with all who surround me. Teach me to treat all that comes to me throughout the day with peace of soul, and with firm convictions that thy will governs all. In all my deeds and words guide my thoughts and feelings. In unforeseen events let me not forget that all are sent by thee. Teach me to act firmly and wisely, without embittering and embarrassing others. Give me strength to bear the fatigue of the coming day with all that it shall bring. Direct my will, teach me to pray, pray thou thyself in me. Amen.

—*Metropolitan Philaret of Moscow, d. 1867*

THOMAS MOORE

January 29, 1999

Mary Reath
Princeton, NJ 08540

Dear Mary Reath,

Thanks for including me on your list of people to include in your book.

It is so difficult to select a single, pointed text,
but this one from Emily Dickinson is one I often call to mind:

Lad of Athens, faithful be
To Thyself
And Mystery
All the rest is Perjury

—Emily Dickinson (1830–1886)

Sincerely,

Thomas Moore

Thomas Moore
Author

Lauren Hutton

Model and Spokeswoman

Probably only this last sentence for brevity's sake, but the entire sentence please, because if the last half is not used, it is only half alive.

"This above all: to thine own self be true,
And it must follow, as the night the day,
Thou canst not then be false to any man."

—*from* Hamlet, *Act I, Scene iii*

JOHN WARNER
VIRGINIA

COMMITTEES
ARMED SERVICES
ENVIRONMENT AND PUBLIC WORKS
RULES AND ADMINISTRATION
LABOR AND HUMAN RESOURCES
SMALL BUSINESS
AGING

United States Senate
October 21, 1998

John Warner

U.S. Senator, Virginia

I approach all of life's challenges with my father's advice foremost in mind. He borrowed words from William Shakespeare and reminded my brother Charles and me to always

"Be true to thine self."

Ms. Mary Reath
Princeton,

Dear Ms. Reath

Thank you for seeking success. It is always a pleasure to receive letters
from those striving to achieve their personal best.

The time I spent in the military had a tremendous impact on my success. Much of
my successes and experiences and lessons learned from serving in the United States Navy
during World War II and the United States Marines during the Korean Conflict have taught me
the remarkable value of liberty and freedom; merits that Americans should never take for
granted.

I approach all of life's challenges with my father's advice foremost in mind. He borrowed
words from William Shakespeare and reminded my brother Charles and I to always 'Be true to
thine self.' I value the guidance offered by my father and cherish the principles that my parents
instilled in me.

I wish you the best of luck with all future endeavors. Thank you for your interest and
inquiry.

With kind regards, I am

Sincerely,

John Warner

John Warner

JW/vjc

20

Howard Fast
Author

*There are a thousand choices, an impossible task, but considering the times,
I like this old favorite of mine:*

The Rabbi Hillel, perhaps the most beloved sage in the Jewish past and a contemporary of Jesus, was approached by a Greek, who said he wanted to become Jewish, but despaired of ever learning the Law——that is, the five books of the Pentateuch. To this, Rabbi Hillel replied, "Love thy neighbor as thyself. That is the whole law. All the rest is commentary."

— Hillel the Elder (ca. 40 B.C.E.–10 C.E.) Talmud, Shabbat 31a

Belva Plain
Author

Do not do unto others that which
you would not have them do unto you.
That is the Law. The rest is commentary.

—Hillel

James B. Hunt

Governor of North Carolina

The Lord's Prayer is my favorite prayer and passage from the Bible. It inspires me every day.

One day Jesus was praying in a certain place. When he finished, one of his disciples said to him, "Lord, teach us to pray, just as John taught his disciples." He said to them, "When you pray, say: 'Father, hallowed be your name, your kingdom come. Give us each day our daily bread. Forgive us our sins, for we also forgive everyone who sins against us. And lead us not into temptation.'"

—Luke 11:1-4

George Kennan
Former State Department Official

How can anyone who recognizes the authority of Christ's teaching and example accept, even as a humble citizen, the slightest share of responsibility for doing this——and not just for doing it, but for even incurring the risk of doing it? This civilization we are talking about is not the property of our generation alone. We are not the proprietor's of it; we are only the custodians. It is something infinitely greater and more important than we are. It is the whole; we are only a part. It is not our achievement; it is the achievement of others. We did not create it. We inherited it. It was bestowed upon us; and it was bestowed upon us with the implicit obligation to cherish it, to preserve it, to develop it, to pass it on——let us hope improved, but in any case intact——to the others who were supposed to come after us.

—from The Nuclear Delusion,
Soviet-American Relations in the Atomic Age,
Pantheon Books, New York, 1982, page 205

The Interfaith Center of New York

P. N. Jain (Bawa)
The Interfaith Center of New York

The sayings I am including are my own, based on the teachings of my spiritual teacher, H. H. Acharya Sushil Kumar Jai Maharaj.

1. Nonviolence is the key to survival.

2. The dawn of nonviolence shall usher in an era of harmonious coexistence where the unifying principles of all religions will become the foundations for world peace.

24

Joan Baez
Singer

I vow to seek the truth, to live by the truth, and to confront the truth wherever I find it.

—*Mohandas Gandhi (1869–1948)*

Malachy McCourt
Author

If you want to give God a good laugh, tell him your future plans.
So do your best and God will do the rest.

Dear Mary,

Thank you for asking me to contribute to your collection.

Here it is:

If you want to give God a good laugh, tell him your future plans. So do your best & God will do the rest.

Blessings

M.

Malachy McCourt
New York, NY 10025

Ann Landers

Advice Columnist

Life by the yard
Is awfully hard,
But by the inch,
It's a cinch.

February 16, 1999

Rev. Darrell Fast

Moderator, General Conference Mennonite Church

Two things fill the mind with ever new and increasing admiration and awe, the oftener and more readily we reflect on them: the starry heavens above me and the moral law within me.

—*Immanuel Kant (1724-1804),*
Critique of Practical Reason

Brooke Astor

Philanthropist and Author

Discipline

I am old and I have had
more than my share of good and bad.
I've had love and sorrow, seen sudden death
and been left alone and of love bereft.
I thought I would never love again
and I thought my life was grief and pain.
The edge between life and death was thin,
but then I discovered discipline.
I learned to smile when I felt sad,
I learned to take the good and bad,
I learned to care a great deal more
for the world about me than before.
I began to forget the "Me" and "I"
and joined in life as it rolled by:
this may not mean sheer ecstasy
but is better by far than "I" and "Me."

—Brooke Astor

September 8, 1998

Dan Coats

U.S. Senator from Indiana

Mary Reath
Princeton, New Jersey

Dear Mary:

I have always found comfort in the words and meaning of the Serenity Prayer.

that has special meaning. I have always
found comfort in the words and meaning of the
Serenity Prayer:

God, grant me the serenity to accept the things I cannot change;
the courage to change the things I can;
and the wisdom to know the difference.

—*Gustave Niebuhr (1892–1971)*

God, grant me the serenity to accept
the things I cannot change;
the courage to change the things I can;
and the wisdom to know the difference.

I hope this information is useful to you in
the production of your book. Please let me know
if I can be of further assistance.

Sincerely,

Dan Coats
U. S. Senator

Monsignor Tom Hartman
AND
Rabbi Marc Gelman

The God Squad, Imus Radio Program

There are different kinds of spiritual gifts but the same Spirit; there are different forms of service but the same Lord; there are different workings but the same God who produces all of them in everyone. To each individual the manifestation of the Spirit is given for some benefit. To one is given through the Spirit the expression of wisdom; to another the expression of knowledge according to the same spirit; to another faith by the same spirit; to another gifts of healing by the one Spirit; to another mighty deeds; to another prophecy; to another discernment of spirits; to another varieties of tongues; to another interpretation of tongues. But one and the same Spirit produces all of these, distributing them individually to each person as he wishes.

—1 Corinthians 12:4-11

Her Majesty Queen Noor
Jordan

Amman
March 1999

Work for life on this earth as if you are to live forever, and
work for the life after in heaven as if you are to die tomorrow.

—*Sayings of the Prophet Mohammed*

"Work for life on this earth as if you are to live forever, and
work for the life after in heaven as if you are to die tomorrow"

Sayings of the Prophet Mohammed

Contribution to an Anthology of Prayers
by Queen Noor of Jordan

chapter two

Loving

Anna Quindlen
Writer and Columnist

When she was dying my mother wrote out the beginning of St. Paul's most famous letter to the Corinthians on an index card in pencil, and it has ever after been a touchstone for my brothers, my sister, and me.

Though I speak with the tongues of men and of angels but have not love, I am a noisy gong or a clanging cymbal.

—1 Corinthians 13:1

Dear Mar...

Well, I have two thoughts right on... The first is... letter to the... mother wrote out the beginning of St. Paul's most... men and of angels... for my Corinthians ("Though I speak with the tongues of men and of angels... been a touchstone for my lover...") card in pencil, and it... read it near the end of one particular... my sister and... you can hear the speech I give... the house always grows... audience breathing.

The other is more pedestrian, but no less persuasive for me: God grant me the serenity to accept the things I cannot change, the courage to change the things I can, and the wisdom to know the difference. It's the AA prayer, and it certainly has legs. I was asked to provide the last word during one of those Fred Friendly media and society roundtables on PBS, this one on death and dying, and that's what I said. People were pretty knocked out. I don't think they expect anyone to pray anymore, much less pray on public television.

Hope Fran and Henry are well. Let me know if you want more.

Best, Anna

Martin Sheen

Actor

Fear is useless
Faith is necessary
Love is everything!

Jane Alexander

Actress

Sometimes——there's God——so quickly!

—*Blanche, in Tennessee Williams'* A Streetcar Named Desire

Ved Mehta

Author

Just short of five, I was sent to what my father thought was a boarding school some thirteen hundred miles away from our home, but which turned out to be an orphanage. I was there for three years, nearly half the time in a hospital, where I fell under the influence of my nurse. I was a Hindu child; she was a Christian, and thanks to her, I became, for want of a better word, a temporary Christian. Here is my first Christian prayer, which has stayed with me now for some fifty-six years. The following is its text.

Heavenly Father, Thou wilt hear me,
Bless Thy loving child tonight.
Through the darkness be Thou near me,
Keep me safe till morning light.
All this day Thy hand hath led me,
And I thank Thee for thy care.
Thou has clothed me, warmed me, fed me,
Listen to my evening prayer.
Let my sins be all forgiven,
Bless the friends I love so well.
Take us all at last to Heaven,
Happy there with Thee to dwell.

Barbara Bush
former First Lady

Mrs. Bush offered this passage from the gospel of Matthew, stating that she opened the Bible to this passage when George Bush was sworn in as President.

Now when he saw the crowds, he went up on a mountainside and sat down. His disciples came to him, and he began to teach them, saying:
"Blessed are the poor in spirit, for theirs is the kingdom of heaven.
Blessed are those who mourn, for they will be comforted.
Blessed are the meek, for they will inherit the earth.
Blessed are those who hunger and thirst for righteousness, for they will be filled.
Blessed are the merciful, for they will be shown mercy.
Blessed are the pure in heart, for they will see God.
Blessed are the peacemakers, for they will be called the sons of God.
Blessed are those who are persecuted because of righteousness, for theirs is the kingdom of heaven.
Blessed are you when people insult you, persecute you and falsely say all kinds of evil against you because of me.
Rejoice and be glad, because great is your reward in heaven, for in the same way they persecuted the prophets who were before you."

—Matthew 5:1-12

Mangosuthu G. Buthelezi
Chairman of Kwa Zulu-Natal's Inkatha Freedom Party

Mr. Buthelezi offered the same passage from Matthew.

It is a privilege for me to share with you and other believers some readings from which I have derived a lot of inspiration and strength in all the difficult experiences which have been my lot in life.

Art Linkletter
Author and Television Personality

After interviewing 27,000 small children over a 26-year period on CBS, I've made the phrase famous: "Kids Say The Darndest Things." That's why I love the part of the Holy Bible where Jesus says:

"Let the little children come to Me, and do not forbid them; for of such is the kingdom of God.

"Assuredly, I say to you, whoever does not receive the kingdom of God as a little child will by no means enter it."

—Mark 10:14-15

AL:lr

38

Sister Helen Prejean, CSJ
Author of Dead Man Walking

We love because He [Jesus] first loved us.
Those who say, "I love God," and hate their brothers or sisters, are liars;
for those who do not love a brother or sister whom they have seen,
cannot love God whom they have not seen.

1 John 19–20

*We love because He [Jesus] first
loved us. Those who say, "I love
God," and hate their brothers or
sisters, are liars; for those who do
not love a brother or sister whom
they have not seen.*

A. M. Rosenthal

September 8, 1998

Columnist and Former Managing Editor, The New York Times

The passage that means the most to me is the one from Hillel. I have quoted it a couple of times in my column and it hangs on the wall of my apartment.

If I am not for myself, who will be?
If I am only for myself, what am I?
If not now, when?

— *Hillel the Elder*

Dear Ms. Reath,

Please forgive me for not responding to your letter sooner but I have been away.

The passage that means the most to me is the one from Hillel. I have quoted it a couple of times in my column and it hangs on my wall in my apartment.

"If I am not for myself, who will be? If I am only for myself, what am I? If not now, when?"

Sincerely,

Henry Louis Gates, Jr.

Author and Chair,
Afro-American Studies Department,
Harvard University

I would like to contribute to your book a quotation from William E. B. Du Bois that has always been meaningful to me:

Freedom is a state of mind: a spiritual unchoking of the wells of human power and superhuman love.

—W. E. B. Du Bois (1868–1963)

The Right Reverend Paul Moore
Retired Episcopal Bishop of New York

*Freedom is at the heart of the Christian faith
because without freedom we could not love, and without love we
could not fulfill our vocation as members of the body of Christ.*

Francine Du Plessix Gray
Author

I offer you the following, from Emily Dickinson:

Love is anterior to life
Posterior to death
Initial of creation and
The exponent of breath.

The Most Reverend Anthony M. Pilla

Bishop of Cleveland, Former President of the National Conference of Catholic Bishops

A Simple Prayer

Lord, make me an instrument of your peace.

Where there is hatred, let me sow love.
Where there is injury, pardon.
Where there is doubt, faith.
Where there is darkness, light.
Where there is sadness, joy.
O Divine Master, grant that
I may not so much seek
To be consoled as to console.
To be understood as to understand.
To be loved as to love.

For it is in giving that we receive.
It is in pardoning that we are pardoned.
It is in dying that we are born to eternal life.

—Attributed to St. Francis of Assisi

Ed McMahon

Television Personality

contributed the same "Simple Prayer" of St. Francis of Assisi.

Victor Borge
Musician and Comedian

A smile is the shortest distance between two people.

Frank Keating

Governor

Frank Keating

Governor of Oklahoma

There is a lovely parable of a man who looked back on his life and saw it as an endless series of footprints in the sand. At times, there were two sets of footprints, side by side, and he remembered these times as happy. At others there was but one set of prints——the times of sadness and pain. He confronted God and asked why He had ceased to walk beside him when he most needed that support.
Why, he wondered, had God abandoned him?
And God answered: "But, my son, those were the times I was carrying you."
He carries us today, cupped gently in his loving hands.

—*from Governor Keating's remarks at the prayer service*
honoring those who died in the Oklahoma City bombing, April 1995

chapter three

Working

Tim Russert

Television and Media Personality

One of my favorites:

Pray as if everything depended on God.
Work as if everything depended upon you.

—St. Ignatius Loyola (1491–1556)

Susanna Agnelli

Roman Politician

What you spend years building may be destroyed overnight—
Build anyway.

George Plimpton
Author

A Latin proverb I rather like:

"When there is no wind, row."

Kemp Battle
Author and Investment Banker

Until one is committed, there is hesitancy,
the chance to draw back, always ineffectiveness.
Concerning acts of initiative (and creation) there is one elementary truth the
ignorance of which kills countless ideas and splendid plans:
That the moment one definitely commits then Providence moves too. All sorts of
things occur to help one that would never have otherwise occurred.
A whole stream of events issues from the decision,
raising in one's favor all manner of unforeseen incidents and meetings and material
assistance which no person could have dreamt would come that way.
Whatever you can do, or dream you can, begin it.
Boldness has genius, power, and magic in it.
Begin it now.

—Goethe

MICKEY SPILLANE PRODUCTIONS

Art and Staging by GEORGE WILSON • Production by SPILLANE

Mickey Spillane
Author

From a teacher in grade school a <u>long</u> time ago!

The man who says it can't be done
is always interrupted by the man
who just did it.

Dan Glickman

U.S. Secretary of Agriculture

When you reap the harvest of your land, you shall not reap
to the very edges of your field, or gather the gleanings of your harvest.
You shall not strip your vineyard bare, or gather the fallen grapes
of your vineyard; you shall leave them for the poor and the alien.

—Leviticus 19:9-10

Kurt L. Schmoke

Former Mayor of Baltimore

Unless the Lord builds the house,
    those who build it labor in vain.
Unless the Lord guards the city,
    the guard keeps watch in vain.

—Psalm 127:1

Robert E. Sawyer

President, Provincial Elder's Conference,
Moravian Church in America

Few of us will have the greatness to bend history, but each of us can work to change
a small portion of events, and in the total of all those acts will
be written the history of this generation.

—*Robert F. Kennedy (1925–1968)*

Provincial Elders' Conference
MORAVIAN CHURCH IN AMERICA
SOUTHERN PROVINCE

Robert E. Sawyer
PRESIDENT

Don Nickles

U.S. Senator, Oklahoma

Seven Steps to a Better Life

1. Get up a half hour earlier than you normally do.
2. Get on your knees and have your quiet time. Express gratitude.
3. Read something positive—the New Testament, Psalms, or Proverbs.
4. Go outside and look around. Breathe deeply and see the beauty. Meditate.
5. Get some exercise and take a quick shower.
6. Eat a good breakfast.
7. Greet everyone you see with love in your heart.

—Don Nickles

GEORGE BUSH

May 12, 1998

Dear Mary,

When I was President of the United States, I discovered firsthand
what Abraham Lincoln meant when he talked about "spending time
on his knees."

Barbara and I regularly attended church services, most of the time
out of the public eye. We loved worshipping in the beautiful little
chapel at Camp David and at our little church, St. Ann's By The Sea
in Kennebunkport. I found that attending church did, indeed, give
me spiritual renewal — give me strength.

Sincerely,

Ms. Mary Reath
Princeton, NJ 08540

George Bush

41st President of the United States

Dear Mary,

When I was President of the United States, I discovered firsthand
what Abraham Lincoln meant when he talked about "spending time on his knees."

Barbara and I regularly attended church services, most of the time out of the
public eye. We loved worshipping in the beautiful little chapel
at Camp David and at our little church, St. Ann's By The Sea in
Kennebunkport. I found that attending church did,
indeed, give me spiritual renewal—give me strength.

Sincerely,
George Bush

Brigitte Bardot
Actress and Activist

Le bruit ne fait pas de bien
Le bien ne fait pas de bruit.

*Noise does not do any good
And good does not make any noise.*

Mary Reath
Princeton NJ 08540
(U S A)

Harold S. Kushner
Rabbi and Author

I have taken as the cornerstone of my faith the verse from Isaiah 40:31:

Those who trust in the Lord will have their strength renewed. They shall mount up with wings as eagles. They shall run and not grow weary, they shall walk and not feel faint.

I don't ask God to give me a life free of problems. I ask God to renew my strength so that I will be up to the challenges, even the unfair ones, that life deals me.

Mario M. Cuomo
FORMER GOVERNOR OF NEW YORK

*The example of my father has been a powerful and lasting influence throughout my life.
I wrote of this in a diary entry during my first campaign for Governor.
The following excerpt is from the collection of entries published in 1984:*

Blue Spruce

Whenever I'm feeling down, I can't help but wonder what Poppa would have said if I had told him I was tired or——God forbid——that I was discouraged. If I think about how he dealt with hard circumstances, a thousand different pictures flash through my mind——he was so used to dealing with hard circumstances. When he and Momma were struggling to raise us, almost everything was hard.

But one scene in particular comes sharply into view.

After living for years in the rooms behind my father's tiny grocery store in the city, we had just moved into our own house for the first time; it had some land around it, even trees——one, in particular, was a great blue spruce that must have been forty feet high.

The neighborhood was hilly. Our house sat ten or fifteen feet above the road itself, and the blue spruce stood majestically like a sentinel at the corner of our property, where the street made a turn, bending around our property line.

Less than a week after we moved in, there was a terrible storm. We came home from the store that night to find the great blue spruce pulled almost totally out of the ground and flung forward, its mighty nose bent in the asphalt of the street. My brother Frankie and I knew nothing about trees. We could climb poles all day; we were great at fire escapes; we could scale fences with barbed wire at the top——but we knew nothing about trees. When we saw our spruce, defeated, its cheek on the canvas, our hearts sank. But not Poppa's.

Maybe he was five feet six if his heels were not worn. Maybe he weighed 155 pounds if he had had a good meal. Maybe he could see a block away if his glasses were clean. But he was stronger than Frankie and me and Marie and Momma all together.

We stood in the street looking down at the tree. The rain was still falling. We waited a couple of minutes for him to figure things out and then he announced, "O.K., we gonna push 'im up!"

"What are you talking about, Poppa? The roots are out of the ground!"

"Shut up, we gonna push 'im up, he's gonna grow again."

We didn't know what to say to him. You couldn't say no to him——not just because you were his son, but because he was so sure.

So we followed him into the house and got what rope there was and we tied the rope around the tip of the tree that lay in the asphalt, and we stood up by the house, with me pulling on the rope and Frankie in the street in the rain, helping to push up the great blue spruce. In no time at all, we had it standing up straight again!

With the rain falling still, Poppa dug away at the place where the roots were, making a muddy hole wider and wider as the tree sank lower and lower toward security. Then we shoveled mud over the roots and moved boulders to the base of the tree to keep it in place. Poppa drove stakes in the ground, tied rope from the trunk to the stakes, and maybe two hours later looked at the spruce, the crippled spruce made straight by ropes, and said, "Don't worry, he's gonna grow again."

If you were to drive past that house today you would see the great, straight blue spruce, maybe sixty-five feet tall, pointing straight up to the heavens, pretending it never had its nose in the asphalt.

And that's how good things happen: Dreams. A little common sense. Perseverance. Courage. Not quitting. And a little help from your family and your teachers.

—The Diaries of Mario Cuomo

James Baker

Former U.S. Secretary of State

When I think back over the hills and valleys of my life, the consistent theme is the one in Psalm 91.

Say to the Lord, "My refuge and my fortress; my God, in whom I trust."

—Psalm 91:2

October 16, 1998

BILL CAMPBELL
MAYOR

Ms. Marv Reath
Princeton, New Jersey 08540

Dear Ms. Reath,

Bill Campbell
Mayor of Atlanta

As the son of a secretary and a janitor, I saw the flames of hatred during our civil rights struggles.
Many years later, I had the privilege of overseeing the flames of freedom of the Olympic torch,
when Atlanta presided over the 100th anniversary of the Olympic Games.
These two experiences, juxtaposed with each other, exemplify the best and the worst of the
human soul. I never forget the former; I live my life by the values of the latter.

Thank you for your letter. Your inspirational writings have been thought provoking. Many great men and women who have come before me have been quoted, and I often draw upon their words of wisdom. As mayor, I am asked to draw upon the flame of freedom to bring the world together, and I am ill-equipped without the words of those who have come before.

In my years as a son, a husband, and a father, I have been able to draw strength from my own past. As the son of a secretary and a janitor, I saw the flames of hatred during our civil rights struggles. Many years later, I had the privilege of overseeing the flames of freedom of the Olympic torch, when Atlanta presided over the 100th anniversary of the Olympic Games.

These two experiences, juxtaposed with each other, exemplify the best and the worst of the human soul. I never forget the former; I live my life by the values of the latter.

I hope that these words will be a welcome addition to your collection. Good luck to you as you continue to gather your inspirational writings.

Sincerely,

Bill Campbell

BC/sg

Thomas R. Carper

Governor of Delaware

1. Do what's right.
2. Do your best.
3. Treat others the way you want them to treat you.
4. Never give up.

August 18, 1998

E. Benjamin Nelson
Governor

Mary Reath
Princeton, NJ 08540

Dear Mary,

Being elected governor was a goal of mine from the time I was a young boy, and I am very proud to have achieved my goal. As Governor of Nebraska, I would like to share with you thoughts and some pieces of advice I have received and some lessons I have learned throughout my life.

E. Benjamin Nelson
Governor of Nebraska

To be a great leader one must possess a sense of responsibility, the importance of vision, problem-solving skills, the ability to take risks, and lastly, the ability to earn the respect and confidence of others. These skills were introduced to me during my early school years, and from there it was up to me to learn to use them and put them to work.

"A good education is like getting a ticket on a train. You can go as far as you want, but you have to pay the fare."

—*Birdella Ruby Nelson, my mother*

Thank you for the invitation to contribute to your book of wisdom. I wish you the best throughout the project and I wish you the best throughout all of your future endeavors.

Sincerely,

E. Benjamin Nelson
Governor

Rabbi Gilbert S. Rosenthal
The New York Board of Rabbis

Schwester Selma Mayer served as a chief nurse of Jerusalem's Shaare Zadek Hospital until her death well into her 90s. Born in Hamburg, Germany, she was orphaned at an early age. She studied nursing and in 1916, took up her duties in Jerusalem. She never married because her duties took up all of her time. She did, however, adopt two orphan daughters. She served her patients through wars and plagues, terrorist attacks and privation. Her favorite poem was by Tagore, the great Bengali poet. It summed up her life's work and philosophy.

I slept and dreamt that life was joy,

I awoke and saw that life was service,

I acted and behold, service was joy.

—Rabindranath Tagore (1861–1941)

Parris N. Glendening
Governor of Maryland

One of my favorite Bible passages is Proverbs 29:18:

"Where there is no vision the people perish."

Edward G. Rendell

Chairman, Democratic Party,
Former Mayor of Philadelphia

The woods are lovely, dark and deep,
But I have promises to keep,
And miles to go before I sleep,
And miles to go before I sleep.

—from Robert Frost, "Stopping By Woods on a Snowy Evening"

Peter R. Kann

Chairman, Dow Jones & Company

I've always liked Kipling's poem "If," which propounds a kind of moral, and practical, philosophy to live by.

If you can keep your head when all about you
Are losing theirs and blaming it on you,
If you can trust yourself when all men doubt you,
But make allowance for their doubting too;
If you can wait and not be tired by waiting,
Or being lied about, don't deal in lies,
Or being hated, don't give way to hating,
And yet don't look too good, nor talk too wise:

If you can dream, and not make dreams your master,
If you can think, and not make thoughts your aim,
If you can meet Triumph and Disaster, and treat those two imposters just the same,
If you can bear to hear the truth you've spoken twisted by knaves
    to make a trap for fools,
Or watch the things you gave your life to, broken, and stoop and build 'em up with
    worn-out tools:

If you can make one heap of all your winnings and risk it
    on one turn of pitch-and-toss,
And lose, and start again at your beginnings and never breathe a word
    about your loss,
If you can force your heart and nerve and sinew to serve your turn
    long after they are gone,

66

And so hold on when there is nothing in you except the Will
which says to them, "Hold on!"

If you can walk with crowds and keep your virtue or walk with Kings,
nor lose the common touch,
If neither foes nor loving friends can hurt you, if all men count with you,
but none too much,
If you can fill the unforgiving minute, with sixty seconds' worth of distance run,
Yours is the Earth and everything that's in it,
And—which is more—you'll be a Man, my son.

—*Rudyard Kipling (1865-1936)*

John A. Kitzhaber, M.D.
G o v e r n o r   o f   O r e g o n

contributed the same Kipling poem.

Allen Gurganus
Author of <u>The Oldest Living Confederate Widow</u>

Blessings on your beautiful enterprise.

A Child's Morning Prayer to the Force of Concentration

Today, give me the world one face at a time. Let me study only what I'm looking at right now. From the trillion images being shot my way for profit, fun, and glut's sake, give me strength, oh Concentrator, to choose one, to find my choice sufficient, to help complete it. Let me, not graze, not drift——but burrow, laser, fuse.

Save me from the pestilence of a faith called "Whatever," called just "Next." Indoctrinate me in Now, in simply mainly This. Let me know that, among your countless franchises, I am one unit entire, whole. I am no less valuable than any of your other scattered addled receivers, with rights no greater than theirs, and no less. Grant me the peace to select, edit and direct. Release me, oh Concentrator, from passive feeding.

Let me view, as an achievement, my own central stillness. Let me see that Power is not simply the largest button on my remote's upper right. Grant me no-charge cable access to my own lavish umbilical center. Let me, and my curiosity, be enough.

Among the five hundred channels, allow my favorite——homebase——to remain sweet funny sexy Channel One, my self turned up to its highest-intensity. Do not make all my joys be rental joys. Be kind, rewind me. I know that I can originate because I concentrate. Always switch me, glad, back to me.

May I forever consider myself the Entertainment.
Amen.

—Allen Gurganus

Cesar Pelli
Architect

Here is a sentence that contains much wisdom.

I returned, and saw under the sun, that the race is not to the swift, nor the battle to the strong, neither yet bread to the wise, nor yet riches to men of understanding, nor yet favor to men of skill; but time and chance happeneth to them all.

—Ecclesiastes 9:11

chapter four

Doubting

The Most Rev. Desmond Tutu

Archbishop Emeritus, Cape Town, South Africa

I hope that a quote from scripture will serve you. Romans 5:1-11 has always moved me deeply and been a source of inspiration.

Therefore, since we are justified by faith, we have peace with God through our Lord Jesus Christ. Through him we have obtained access to this grace in which we stand, and we rejoice in our hope of sharing glory with God.
More than that, we rejoice in our sufferings, knowing that suffering produces endurance, and endurance produces character, and character produces hope, and hope does not disappoint us, because God's love has been poured into our hearts though the Holy Spirit which has been given to us.
While we were still weak, at the right time Christ died for the ungodly.
Why, one will hardly die for a righteous man—
though perhaps for a good man one will dare even to die.
But God shows his love for us in that while we were yet sinners Christ died for us.
Since, therefore, we are now justified by his blood, much more shall we be saved by him from the wrath of God.
For if while we were enemies we were reconciled to God by the death of his Son, much more, now that we are reconciled, shall we be saved by his life.
Not only so, but we also rejoice in God through our Lord Jesus Christ, through whom we have now received our reconciliation.

—Romans 5:1-11

September 1, 1998

Rev. Theodore M. Hesburgh, C.S.C.

President Emeritus, University of Notre Dame

I think one of the largest problems in life generally, and in the spiritual life in particular, is what to do when one comes to a spiritual or moral crossroads. Part of the problem is to have the courage to do what one should, but an even deeper problem is to know what one should do.

Life is often perplexing.

The greatest help I have found in this regard is a three word prayer, "Come, Holy Spirit." No matter what the problem, I have always found that this brief prayer brings two great graces: first, the light to see and, second, the strength to act as one should. I can't think of anything else that has been more helpful in life and I am happy to share it with others who are perplexed at times, as we all are.

I think one of the largest problems in life generally, and in the spiritual life in particular, is what to do when one comes to a spiritual or moral crossroads. Part of the problem is to have the courage to do what one should, but an even deeper problem is to know what one should do. Life is often perplexing.

The greatest help I have found in this regard is a three word prayer, "Come, Holy Spirit." No matter what the problem, I have always found that this brief prayer brings two great graces; first the light to see and, secondly, the strength to act as one should. I can't think of anything else that has been more helpful in life and I am happy to share it with others who are perplexed at times, as we all are.

Ever devotedly in Notre Dame,

(Rev.) Theodore M. Hesburgh, C.S.C.
President Emeritus

Evan Thomas

Author and Assistant Managing Editor of Newsweek

Courage is not simply one of the virtues but the form of every virtue at the testing point.

—C. S. Lewis (1898-1963)

Rt. Rev. Lord Robert Runcie (1922-2000)

Former Archbishop of Canterbury

Religion is so noble and powerful a consideration, it is buoyant and insubmergible, that it may be made, by fanatics, to carry with it any degree of error and of serious absurdity.

—Sidney Smith, Canon of St. Paul's Cathedral, in the Edinburgh Review 1808

Seamus Heaney

Poet and Nobel Laureate

The Angel that presided o'er my birth

The Angel that presided o'er my birth
Said, 'Little Creature form'd of Joy and Mirth,
Go love without the help of any Thing on Earth.'

—William Blake (1757-1827)

Jonathan Sacks

Office of the Chief Rabbi, London

We who lived in concentration camps can remember men who walked through the huts comforting others, giving away their last piece of bread. They may have been few in number, but they offer sufficient proof that everything can be taken away from a man but one thing: the last of human freedoms——to choose one's attitude in any given set of circumstances, to choose one's own way.

—Viktor E. Frankl (1905-1998)

Rt. Rev. Richard F. Grein
Bishop of the Episcopal Diocese of New York

I have kept a copy of this brief prayer (Saint Teresa's Bookmark) on my desk ever since I was consecrated as a Bishop. I have found that it helps me keep focused in the midst of the turmoil that accompanies this office as it reminds me that my relationship with God is the only thing that ultimately matters.

Let nothing disturb you,
Nothing frighten you—
All things pass,
But God never changes.
Patient endurance attains all things,
He who possesses God
is wanting in nothing—
God alone is enough.

—*St. Teresa of Avila*

Faithfully in Christ,

+ Richard

Richard F. Grein
Bishop of New York

Julie Harris
Actress

also submitted St. Teresa of Avila's prayer.

Carl Lewis

Olympic Track Star

Every word of God proves true:
he is a shield to those who
take refuge in him.

—*Proverbs 30:5*

Marc Racicot

Governor of Montana

In any moment of decision the best thing you can do is the right thing, the next best
thing is the wrong thing, and the worst thing you can do is nothing.

—*Theodore Roosevelt (1858-1919)*

Rita Mae Brown
Author

If you want the honest *spiritual truth, my prayer is this:*

Dear God, get me out of this mess.

Sue Bender
Author, Plain and Simple

Small miracles are all around us. We can find them everywhere—in our homes, in our daily activities, and, hardest to see, in ourselves.
To be WHOLE—doesn't mean we have to be perfect.

Danielle Steel
Author

There are indeed a few "standbys" that are what I hang on to In hard times.
Isaiah 41:1 is a favorite of mine:

Fear thou not; for I am with thee: be not dismayed: for I am thy God:
I will strengthen thee; yea I will help thee;
yea, I will uphold thee with the right hand of my righteousness.

And Isaiah 41:13:
For I the Lord thy God will hold thy right hand, saying unto thee,
Fear not: I will help thee.

The 91st Psalm is also one of my favorites.
And there is a saying in my church, which is also very helpful:

Divine Love always has met and always will meet every human need

(from Mary Baker Eddy, Science and Health*).*

The "always has" and "always will" and "every" are particularly reassuring.
I always seem to find what I need in the Bible, and in the Lord's Prayer as well. I hope these are
what you had in mind. Pretty basic, and not too exciting, but always there,
always reliable, always comforting.

Al Green
Gospel Singer

"These things I have spoken unto you, that in me ye might have peace. In the world ye shall have tribulation, but be of good cheer, for I have overcome the world."

—*John 16:33*

Robert S. Folkenberg
President, Seventh Day Adventist Church

". . . him that cometh to me I will in no wise cast out."

—*John 6:37*

If you have nothing else to plead before God but this one promise from your Lord and Savior, you have the assurance that you will never, never be turned away. It may seem to you that you are hanging on a single promise, but appropriate that one promise, and it will open to you the whole treasure house of the riches of the grace of Christ. Cling to that promise and you are safe. "Him that cometh unto me I will in no wise cast out."

—*Ellen White*

Laurence Luckinbill

Actor

These are words I try to live by.

Maybe justice doesn't exist, and maybe it doesn't matter. Maybe the only thing that matters is that if we realize our common suffering and our common need, it will bring us not a desire for justice, but only a desire to help in this world, in proportion to our strength. . . . I am pleading for a time when hatred and cruelty will not control the hearts of men, I am pleading for a time when we will have learned by reason and judgment and understanding that all life is worth saving, and that the highest attribute of man is mercy.

Clarence Darrow (1857–1938)

George Rupp

President, Columbia University

And now, O Lord, what do I wait for?
My hope is in you.
Deliver me from all my transgressions. Do not make me the scorn of the fool.
I am silent; I do not open my mouth, for it is you who have done it.
Remove your stroke from me;
I am worn down by the blows of your hand.

You chastise mortals in punishment for sin;
consuming like a moth what is dear to them;
surely everyone is a mere breath.

Hear my prayer, O Lord, and give ear to my cry;
do not hold your peace at my tears.
For I am your passing guest, an alien, like all my forebears.

—Psalm 39:7-12

Rita Dove

Former U.S. Poet Laureate

A companion on this journey:

When you try to stay on the surface of the water, you sink;
but when you try to sink, you float.

—*Zen proverb*

September 18, 1998

Kathleen Norris
Author

... *a passage from my favorite psalm.*

Of you my heart has spoken:
Seek God's face.

It is your face, O Lord, that I seek;
hide not your face.
Dismiss not your servant in anger;
you have been my help.

Do not abandon or forsake me,
O God my help!
Though father and mother forsake me,
the Lord will receive me.

—*Psalm 27:7-10*

Mary Reath
Princeton, New Jersey 08540

Dear Mary,

Thank you so much for the lovely booklet. It is a treasure . . . Here is what I've decided to send you, a passage from my favorite psalm:

Of you my heart has spoken:
Seek God's face.

It is your face, O Lord, that I seek;
hide not your face.
Dismiss not your servant in anger;
you have been my help.

Do not abandon or forsake me,
O God my help!
Though father and mother forsake me,
the Lord will receive me.

Ps. 27: 7-10, from The Psalms: Grail Translation from the Hebrew. Chicago: GIA Publications, 1980.

Kathleen Norris

Frederick Buechner

Author

Christ be with you and within you,
Christ behind you, Christ before you,
Christ beside you, Christ to win you.
Christ to comfort and restore you.
Christ beneath you, Christ above,
Christ in quiet and in danger,
Christ with everyone you love,
Christ make you Christ to friend and stranger.

The above is my own adaptation of a prayer ascribed to Saint Patrick ("Saint Patrick's Breastplate," as it is sometimes called).

—Frederick Buechner

Jeannette Sanger
Publisher

I am enclosing a prayer that is part of my weekly meditation group with Mayot Wilkie. I find it very comforting and am enclosing the Tibetan also. We repeat it three times.

The Four Immeasurables

sem chen tham.che de.wa dang de.wa gyu dang den.par gyur chig
sem.chen tham.che dug.ngal dang dung.ngal gyi gyu dang del.war gyur chig
sem.chen tham.che dug.ngal meh.pa de.wa dang mi.del.war gyur chig
sem.chen tham.che nye ring chag dang nyi dang del.wa tang.nyom la na par gyur chig

May all sentient beings attain happiness and the cause of happiness.
May all sentient beings be free from sorrow and the cause for sorrow.
May all sentient beings never be free from the happiness that knows no sorrow.
May all sentient beings abide in equanimity free from feeling near or far,
attachment or aversion.

Joan Armatrading
Singer and Composer

We see things not as they are but as we are.

—Attributed to Dr. Albert Ellis, a founder of Behavior Therapy

Don Sundquist
Governor of Tennessee

I will lift up mine eyes unto the hills from whence cometh my help.
My help cometh from the Lord.

—Psalm 121:1-2

Jim Geringer
Governor of Wyoming

Create in me a clean heart, O God,
And put a new and right spirit within me.
Do not cast me away from your presence,
And do not take your holy spirit from me.
Restore to me the joy of your salvation,
And sustain in me a willing spirit.

—Psalm 51:10-12

Jerry Lewis
Actor

I think this says it all.

Each new day is a gift . . .
That's why it's called the present.
. . . And each tomorrow is another
present we haven't unwrapped yet!

—*Spencer Johnson*, The Perfect Present

Rev. Mary Moore Gaines

Rector, St. James' Episcopal Church, San Francisco

My oldest favorite is a quote from P. T. Barnum (of circus fame) which I kept in my wallet for years and always said that if I were going to have a tombstone, this would be on it.

More persons, on the whole, are hum-bugged by
not believing enough than by believing too much.

—*P. T. Barnum (1810-1891)*

Galway Kinnell

Poet

If your eyes are not deceived by the mirage
Do not be proud of the sharpness of your understanding;
It may be your freedom from this optical illusion
Is due to the imperfectness of your thirst.

—*Sohrawardi (1155-1191)*

Commissioner Robert A. Watson

National Commander of the Salvation Army

Wind can be _enemy_ or _energy_, depending very much on one's perspective. Life's storms can make us stronger in our faith if we trust God and His beautiful promise,

"... My grace is sufficient for thee."

—2 Corinthians 12:9

Edward Idris Cardinal Cassidy

President, Pontifical Council for Promoting Christian Unity

I have given some thought to your request and have come up with quite a few suggestions. Finally, the one that keeps coming back is probably most suitable for someone in the twilight of life and is taken from Psalm 130.

Out of the depths I cry to you, O Lord,
Lord hear my voice.
If you O Lord, should mark our guilt,
Lord who would survive?
But with you is found forgiveness:
And for that we revere you.
Because with the Lord there is mercy
And fullness of redemption.

—Psalm 130:1, 3-4, 7-8

Dale Evans Rogers

Cow Girl Star

I have had some pretty rough trails since the day I gave my life to Jesus Christ—but he has always, through his Holy Spirit, been there for me. I have claimed this promise from Hebrews 13:5.

He hath said:
I will never leave thee, nor forsake thee.

—Hebrews 13:5

George E. Pataki
Governor of New York

My mother often used this phrase and it has become one of my favorites.

Ever in the strife of your own thoughts, obey the nobler impulse.

Julian Bond
Chairman, NAACP

Fight On!

chapter five

Dying

General Convention The Swedenborgian Church

Rev. Edwin G. Capon

Rev. Edwin G. Capon

Past President, General Convention, The Swedenborgian Church

Death took me by the hand and whispered, "Live, for I am coming."

—*Latin Proverb*

Rabbi Alexander M. Schlindler

President Emeritus, Union of American Hebrew Congregations

Perhaps the enclosed, penned by a colleague of mine will serve your need. His liturgical lines evoke a responsive chord within me, especially in moments devoted to the memory of those who were dear to me and who have reached their horizon and are gone out of sight.

Birth is a beginning
And death a destination.
And life is a journey:
From childhood to maturity
And youth to age;
From innocence to awareness
And ignorance to knowing;
And then, perhaps, to wisdom;
From weakness to strength
Or strength to weakness—
And often back again;
From health to sickness
And back, we pray, to health again;
From offense to forgiveness
From loneliness to love,
From joy to gratitude,
From pain to compassion,

And grief to understanding—
From fear to faith;
From defeat to defeat to defeat—
Until, looking backward or ahead,
We see that victory lies
Not at some high place along the way,
But in having made the journey, stage by stage,
A sacred pilgrimage.
Birth is a beginning
And death a destination.
And life is a journey,
A sacred pilgrimage—
To life everlasting.

—*Rabbi Alvin I. Fine,* Gates of Repentance

27 August 1998

Dame Margaret Thatcher
Former Prime Minister of Great Britain

Thou, O Lord, that stillest the raging of the sea, hear, hear us and save us, that we perish not.

O blessed Saviour, that didst save thy disciples ready to perish in a storm, hear us, and save us, we beseech thee.

—*Short Prayers in Respect of a Storm, from* The Book of Common Prayer

The Honorable Thomas H. Kean

President, Drew University;
Former Governor of New Jersey

At Night

O Lord, support us all the day long, until the shadows
lengthen and the evening comes, and the busy world
is hushed, and the fever of life is over, and our work is
done. Then in thy mercy grant us a safe lodging, and a
holy rest, and peace at the last. Amen.

O God, who art the life of mortal men, the light of
the faithful, the strength of those who labour,
and the repose of the dead; We thank thee for the
timely blessings of the day, and humbly supplicate
thy merciful protection all this night. Bring us, we
beseech thee, in safety to the morning hours; through
him who died for us and rose again, thy Son, our
Savior Jesus Christ. Amen.

—*A Family Prayer,* The Book of Common Prayer

Lord Yehudi Menuhin (1916-2000)

Composer and Conductor

My Prayer

To Thee Whom I do not and cannot know——within me and beyond me——and to Whom I am bound by love, fear and faith——to the One and to the Many——I address this prayer:

Guide me to my better self——help me make myself into one who is trusted by living things, creatures and plants, as well as the air, water, earth and light that sustain these, keep me as one who repects the mystery and the character of every variety of life in both its uniqueness and its mass, for all life is essential to its own survival.

Help me to preserve my capacity for wonder, ecstasy and discovery, allow me everywhere to awaken the sense of beauty, and with and for others, we hear, we smell, taste or touch or are otherwise aware of through mind and spirit; help me never to lose the life-giving exercise of protecting all that breathes and thirsts and hungers; all that suffers.

Help me find the zeal to fulfill with both modesty and assurance the various roles I may be called on to play——of teacher, of leader, of student, of missionary, of healer, of friend, of servant, of master. Help me to remain prepared to face the difficult, the painful and the unexpected, to remember the deaf and the blind, the sick and the suffering. Help me to accept Thy ultimate will with resignation and a measure of curiosity; help me to make the best use of adversity and denial.

Help me find a balance between the longer rewards and the shorter pleasures, while remaining in tune with relative values, while patiently according the passage of time its rich harvest of loyalties, experience, achievement, support, and inspiration.

Help me be a good trustee for the body You gave me. No life is to do with as I will, not even my "own," for it is like an object entrusted into "my" temporary keeping, to bequeath back into the earthly cycle in the best possible condition for other life to continue.

Therefore, Thy will be done.

May those who survive me not mourn but continue to be as helpful, kind and wise to others as they were to me. Although I would love to enjoy some years yet the fruits of my lucky and rich life, with my precious wife, family, music, friends, literature, and many projects, in this world of diverse cultures and peoples I have already received such blessing, affection, and protection as would satisfy a thousand lives.

Allow me to see and to feel and to try to ponder and to understand the relationship of the unity of the trinity in all its manifestations.

Help me in all confrontations to see the "trialogue" as opposed to the "dialogue." Help me so that I may decide wisely on such apportionment of pleasure and pain as may fall within my jurisdiction.

And finally, whilst begging Thee to protect me from anger and condemnation, my own of others and others of mine, allow me unpunished to indulge in my particular aversions: Those who would exploit or corrupt for the sake or the abuse of power or money or self-indulgence——for want of a higher mode of satisfaction; from the petty bureaucrat to the ignorant and prejudiced; help them see and confess to You in themselves the error of their ways.

Enlighten them and me and help us to forgive each other.

Also with such enemies as I may possibly have, help me distinguish between the reconcilable and the irreconcilable, encourage me to seek by every means understanding with the one whilst rendering the other ineffective, to learn from both and not deliberately to antagonize either.

Grant me the inspiration you have provided humanity and encourage me to revere and to follow those living examples who enshrine your spirit—— the spirit within and beyond each of us——the spirit of the One and the Many——the illumination of Christ, of Buddha, of Lao-Tse, and of the prophets, sages, philosophers, poets, writers, painters, sculptors, all creators and artists, and all the selfless people, the saints and the mothers, the known and unknown, the exalted and the humble, men, women, children, of all times and all places—— whose spirit and example remain with us and in us forever.

—Yehudi Menuhin

Donna Shalala
U.S. Secretary of Health and Human Services

"A friend sent me this Edwin Arnold poem when my beloved dog died.

Farewell, master, yet not farewell
where I go, ye too shall dwell
I am gone, before your face
A moment's time, a little space
When ye come where I have stepped
Ye will wonder why you wept.

—*Edwin Arnold (1832-1904)*

YOGI BERRA

Dear Mary

10-18-98

Time gets by quickly, life gets away
and, we don't have enough time to do
the things we would like to do.
"It gets too late too early"

Yogi Berra
Baseball Hero

Time gets by quickly, life gets away from us, and we don't have enough time to do all the things we would like to do. "It gets too late too early," just like it did in the outfield at Yankee Stadium.

Bill Graves

Governor of Kansas

As a teenager, I often participated in sports activities at the YMCA in my hometown of Salina, KS. During those years, posted on the wall of the Y, was a famous quote from 1920s sportswriter Grantland Rice. This quote is one that I will never forget:

When the One Great Scorer comes to write against your name——
He marks——not that you won or lost——but how you played the game.

These words had a significant impact on my life. They still do. To this day, these words guide my approach to governing——I believe in an unselfish team concept molded by faith, confidence, and character.

Len Coleman

Former President of the National Baseball League

As you know, I am happiest on the front lines. Thus, it may not come as a surprise that I always think of St. Paul's words:

I have fought the good fight, I have finished the race, I have kept the faith. From now on, there is reserved for me the crown of righteousness, which the Lord, the righteous judge, will give me on that day.

—Timothy 4:7-8

Robert Pinsky
Former Poet Laureate, U.S.A.

CÆLICA - LXXXIII

You that seek what life is in death,
Now find it air that once was breath;
New names unknown, old names gone;
Till time end bodies, but souls none.
Reader! then make time, while you be,
But steps to your eternity.

—*Fulke Greville (1554–1628)*

Lincoln Almond
Governor of Rhode Island

O God our help in ages past,
Our hope for years to come,
Our shelter from the stormy blast,
And our eternal home.

—*Isaac Watts (1674 1748)*

Lynn Redgrave

Actress

While not exactly a sacred text, the following words by Shakespeare have often given me comfort.

Give sorrow words: the grief that does not speak
Whispers the o'er-fraught heart and bids it break.

—Macbeth: *Malcolm: Act IV, Scene iii*

Kent Conrad

U.S. Senator, North Dakota

Enclosed you will find words of an Irish text that I was honored to use in my euology at the funeral of my close friend and chief of staff. I can only hope that by including this writing in your book, it will be an inspiration to others, that a life lived in love and laughter is a life that is complete.

Death is nothing at all——
I have only slipped away into the next room.
Whatever we were to each other, that we are still.
Call me by my old familiar name. Speak to me in the easy way we always used.
I am but waiting for you, for an interval, somewhere very near, just around the corner.
All is well. Nothing is passed. Nothing is lost.
One brief moment, and all will be as it was before,
only better, happier, and forever.

—from a Carmelite Monastery in Ireland

Paul Scofield
A c t o r

*I enclose the beginning of a prayer written by Thomas More, and given to me when I was
attempting to portray him in the play* A Man for All Seasons *in New York in 1962. I was there
for nine months and beginning to feel a home-sickness, and oddly enough, in that city,
a certain loneliness. This prayer helped me.*

Give me thy grace, good Lord, to set the world at nought;
To set my mind fast upon thee, and not to hang upon the blast of men's mouths;
To be content to be solitary;
Not to long for wordly company;
Little and little utterly to cast off the world, and rid my mind
of the business thereof.

*—Part of a prayer written by St. Thomas More
in the margin of his prayer book, while imprisoned.*

chapter six

Adoring

Sri Chinmoy
Religious Leader

I wish to offer an unparalleled prayer from the Upanishads. This prayer has been ringing in the firmament of India for many centuries:

Asato mā sad gamaya
Lead me from the unreal to the Real.

Tamaso mā jyotir gamaya
Lead me from darkness to Light.

Mṛtyor mā amṛtaṃ gamaya
Lead me from death to Immortality.

Dave Brubeck

Jazz Artist

Iroquois Prayer

We return thanks: to our mother, the earth, which sustains us.
We return thanks: to the rivers and streams, which supply us with water.
We return thanks: to all herbs, which furnish the cure for our diseases.
We return thanks: to the corn, and to her sisters,
the beans and squashes, which give us life.
We return thanks: to the bushes and trees, which provide us with fruit.
We return thanks: to the wind, which, moving the air, has banished disease.
We return thanks: to the moon and stars,
which have given us their light when the sun was gone.
We return thanks: to the sun, that he looked upon the earth with a beneficent eye.
Lastly, we return thanks: to the Great Spirit, who is embodied in all goodness.

—*Translation by Ely S. Parker*

Sister Joan Kirby, R.S.C.J.
Temple of Understanding, New York City

This is a succinct way to sum up our spiritual aspirations gone astray for whatever reasons. I like the directness of the style.

The Buddha Capable of Great Penetrating Knowledge

A monk asked Master Rang of Xingyang, "The Buddha Capable of Great Penetrating Knowledge sat on the site of enlightenment for ten eons, but the realities of enlightenment did not become apparent to him, and he was unable to fulfill the way of Buddhahood. Why was that?"
The master said, "Your question is quite clearly to the point."
The monk said, "Since he was sitting on the site of enlightenment, why was he unable to fulfill the way of Buddhahood?"
The master said, "Because he did not fulfill Buddhahood."

—Koan 9: from the Buddhist Mumonkan in
Unlocking the Zen Koan. *Translated by Thomas Cleary.*

Pete Seeger
Singer

Every time I'm out under the sky, I know I'm in church.

Wendy Wasserstein
Playwright

Oddly, I renew myself spiritually at the ballet. There is something uplifting, startlingly clear, and triumphant in the human perfection of a beautifully danced Balanchine ballet.

I am, at that time, at peace and in awe.

The Rt. Rev. and Hon. George Carey

Archbishop of Canterbury

Prayer

Prayer the Churches banquet, Angels age,
    God's breath in man returning to his birth,
    The soul in paraphrase, heart in pilgrimage,
The Christian plummet sounding heav'n and earth;

Engine against th' Almightie, sinners towre,
    Reversed thunder, Christ-side-piercing spear,
    The six-daies-world transposing in an houre,
A kinde of tune, which all things heare and fear;

Softnesse, and peace, and joy, and love, and blisse,
    Exalted Manna, gladnesse of the best,
    Heaven in ordinarie, man well drest,
The milkie may, the bird of Paradise,
    Church-bels beyond the starres heard, the souls bloud,
    The land of spices; something understood.

—*George Herbert (1593-1633)*

Here is one of my favorites. The Bright Prayer is called An Phaidir Gheal in Gaelic, and is similar in many ways to the White Pater Noster in medieval English literature.

The Bright Prayer

I lie with God
may He lie with me.
God's shade above me,
an angel-girdle around my waist.
Where will you lie tonight?
Between Mary and her Son
between Bridget and her cloak
between Colm Cille and his shield
between God and His right hand.
Where will you rise tomorrow?
I will rise with Patrick.
Who are those before us?
Two hundred angels.
Who are those behind us?
The rest of God's people.
Close the ramparts on Hell
and open God's heavenly gate.
Let the great light out,
let the wretched soul in.
God have mercy upon us.
Son of the Virgin, receive our souls.

Oifig an Taoisigh
Office of the Taoiseach

24 September, 1998.

Ms. Mary Reath,
Princeton,
NJ 08540.

Dear Ms. Reath,

Many thanks for your interesting request for my favourite spiritual reading. and texts. I wish you every success with your work and I hope to read it when it is published. Here is one of my favourite prayers, which is in it when it is published. Here is one of my favourite prayers, which is in

It is called *An Phaidir Gheal* in Gaelic, The Bright Prayer, and is similar in many ways to the White Pater Noster in medieval English literature.

Yours sincerely,

Bertie

Bertie Ahern, T.D.,
Taoiseach.

113

Robert C. Byrd

U.S. Senator, West Virginia

Touch of the Master's Hand

'Twas battered and scarred, and the auctioneer
Thought it scarcely worth his while
To waste much time on the old violin,
But held it up with a smile.
"What am I bidden, good folks," he cried,
"Who will start bidding for me?
A dollar, a dollar—" then, "Two!" "Only two?
Two dollars, and who'll make it three?
Three dollars once; three dollars, twice;
Going for three—" But no,
From the room, far back, a gray-haired man
Came forward and picked up the bow;
Then, wiping the dust from the old violin,
And tightening the loose strings,
He played a melody pure and sweet,
As sweet as a caroling angel sings.

The music ceased, and the auctioneer,
With a voice that was quiet and low,
Said, "What am I bidden for the old violin?"
And he held it up with the bow.
"A thousand dollars, and who'll make it two?
Two thousand! And who'll make it three?

Three thousand, once; three thousand, twice;
And going, and gone!" said he.
The people cheered, but some of them cried,
"We do not quite understand
What changed its worth?" Swift came the reply:
"The touch of the master's hand."

And many a man with life out of tune,
And battered and scattered with sin,
Is auctioned cheap to the thoughtless crowd,
Much like the old violin.
A "mess of pottage," a glass of wine;
A game—and he travels on.
He's "going" once, and "going" twice,
He's "going" and almost "gone."
But the Master comes, and the foolish crowd
Never can quite understand
The worth of a soul, and the change that's wrought
By the touch of the Master's hand.

—Myra Brooks Welch

114

The Rt. Rev. Frank T. Griswold

Presiding Bishop of the Episcopal Church

Father,
I abandon myself into your hands;
Do with me what you will
Whatever you may do,
I thank you.
I am ready for all,
I accept all.
Let only your will
be done in me,
and in all your creatures.
I wish no more than this,
O Lord.

Into your hands
I commend my soul;
I offer it to you
with all the love of my heart,
for I love you, Lord,
and so need to give myself,
to surrender myself
into your hands,
without reserve,
and with boundless confidence,
for you are my Father.

—*Brother Charles of Jesus*

Rev. Dr. John C. Polkinghorne

Anglican Priest and Professor of Mathematical Physics at Cambridge University

The Elixir

Teach me, my God and King,
in all things Thee to see;
and what I do in anything
to do it all for thee.
A man that looks on glass,
on it may stay his eye;
or if he pleases, through it pass,
and then the heaven espy.
All may of thee partake;
nothing can be so mean
which with this tincture, For thy sake,
will not grow bright and clean.
A servant with this clause
makes drudgery divine;
who sweeps a room, as for thy laws,
makes this and the action fine.
This is that famous stone
that turneth all to gold;
for that which God doth touch and own
cannot for less be told.

—*George Herbert (1593–1633)*

John MacQuarrie
Author and Theologian at Oxford University

Teach me, my God and King
In all things Thee to see.

—*George Herbert (1593-1633)*

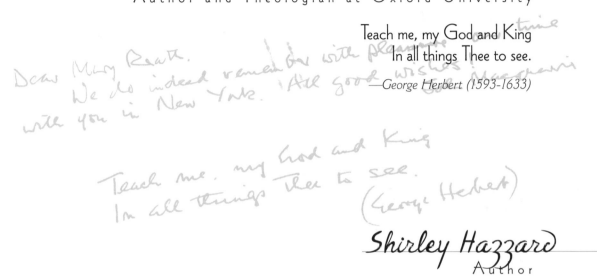

Dear Mary Beth.
We do indeed remember with pleasure the time with you in New York. All good wishes ⟨...⟩ MacQuarrie

Teach me, my God and King
In all things Thee to see.
(George Herbert)

Shirley Hazzard
Author

Any poem by George Herbert.

Genevieve Bujold
Actress

Thy will be done.

Sir John M. Templeton
Investor and Philanthropist

I attribute a large part of my own formula for success to the power of prayer in my daily life. In fact, I begin all my shareholders' and directors' meetings with a prayer. Whatever you do in life, whether you get married, bring a case to court of law, perform surgery on a child, or buy a stock, it is wise to begin with a prayer. That prayer should be that God may use you as a clear channel for his wisdom and love.

The four words, "thy will be done," are probably the most difficult and yet the most important part of any prayer.

Dr. M. G. Prasad

Hindu Temple and Cultural Society of U.S.A.

I offer my deepest gratitude to my Guru Sriranga, a yogi-seer (from Karnataka, India) for the initiation, grace and spiritual guidance, which is the source of my spiritual strength. He is the guiding inspiration for my pursuit of "Seeing the Play of Atman (Universal Soul)." The following poem is a humble expression of mine in the spiritual journey.

I

Pleasure and pains are because of I and mine.
What is this I? And Who am I? And What is mine?
From when did I start feeling this I, I wonder!
I feel the past, present and future but, still I ponder.
Is it that I exist all the time and everywhere,
And for sometime I get this mind and body of I.
Why not I means infinity? Not just me or anyone.
Why is it that I do not fully understand me.
But, eager to understand he and she.
Is it the same I in me and we?
If not, let the I in we become I in me.
Oh! God, show me the I, as only you can,
Because, I was born and You are the Creator.

January 11, 1999

Dr. Ronald B. Sobel

Senior Rabbi, Congregation Emanu-El

Thou who hearest prayer, we beseech Thee to endow us with a contented disposition. When we pray for new blessings, may we come to Thee in the spirit of humility and submission, remembering that we cannot know whether what we ask is really for our good. Thou alone knowest and orderest all things well, whether Thou grantest our petitions or deniest them. When we sing Thy praise, may our souls rise with our songs to Thee, and when we render Thee our homage, may we remember that only by obedience to Thy commandments, by faithfulness to our duties, by the goodness of our deeds, can we make our worship acceptable to Thee.

—Union Prayer Book, *Volume I*

Ms. Mary Reath
Princeton, N.J. 08540

Dear Ms. Reath:

I hope that the holiday season was a time of comfort for you and your family and that the new year will bring to you and to those whom you love an abundance of most precious blessings.

In response to your invitation to record a prayer that has special meaning for me, I submit the following:

"Thou who hearest prayer, we beseech Thee to endow us with a contented disposition. When we pray for new blessings, may we come to Thee in the spirit of humility and submission, remembering that we cannot know whether what we ask is really for our good. Thou alone knowest and orderest all things well, whether Thou grantest our petitions or deniest them. When we sing Thy praise, may our souls rise with our songs to Thee, and when we render Thee our homage, may we remember that only by obedience to Thy commandments, by faithfulness to our duties, by the goodness of our deeds, can we make our worship acceptable to Thee."

From the Union Prayer Book, Volume I.

Thank you for asking me to participate in this wonderful compilation that you are making possible.

Yours sincerely,

Ronald B. Sobel

August 24, 1998

Dear Ms. Reath,

Many things come to mind, and some more obvious than this, but I would like to send you a poem, and it is one that comes to my mind as often and as generously as any I know, modest as it seems to be. It's certainly one that I treasure and return to for just about every reason including those you mention.

Proud Songsters

The thrushes sing as the sun is going,
And the finches whistle in ones and pairs,
And as it gets dark loud nightingales
                    In bushes
Pipe, as they can when April wears,
As if all Time were theirs.

These are brand-new birds of twelve-months' growing,
Which a year ago, or less than twain,
No finches were, nor nightingales,
                    Nor thrushes,
But only particles of grain,
And earth, and air, and rain.

—*Thomas Hardy (1840–1928)*

I hope it will seem appropriate.

Sincerely,

Rodney E. Slater
U.S. Secretary of Transportation

. . . A phrase I viewed on the gravestone of a family friend, noted author of Roots, *Alex Haley, describes the essence of life. It reads,*

Find the good and praise it.

Lawrence S. Huntington
Chairman, Fiduciary Trust International

I have thought some length about the proper submission for you and have realized that the prayer which I love the most is simple, and we hear it all the time.

Oh Lord, take our hearts and set them on fire.

Every time I hear that phrase, I am stirred.

Bo Polk

Investor, Poet, and Former President of MGM

My Creed

I believe in one God.
In one holy and universal church
In the communion of Saints
The forgiveness of Sins
The rejection of violence
The power of evil
The nurturing of love
The need for prayer
The pervasiveness of fear
The disease of greed
The caring family
The gift of freedom
and the message of Christ.

The Rt. Rev. Nathaniel Popp

Bishop of Detroit and The Romanian Orthodox Episcopate of America

October 8, 1998

Mary Reath
Princeton NJ 08540

Among the prayers which have sustained me and kept me in the light of the Way is the following ancient prayer attributed to Saint Efrem of Syria. It is a prayer recited constantly during services of the Great and Holy Forty Day pre-Paschal Fast.

The three verses are interrupted by three physical prostrations, i.e., one kneels and then bows one's head to the floor, arising and repeating the gesture after each verse.

O Lord and Master of my life!
Remove from me the spirit of sadness, despair, thirst for power, and vain talk.
(Prostration)

Instead, grant me your servant, the spirit of prudence, humility, patience, and love.
(Prostration)

Indeed, O Lord and King, grant that I see my own sins and not judge my brother.
Blessed are you unto ages. Amen.
(Prostration)

This is a prayer known and recited by millions of Orthodox Christians around the world and in numerous languages. It is part of the formal worship of the Church.

With all good wishes for your efforts,

+Nathaniel

+NATHANIEL, Bishop of Detroit & The Romanian Orthodox Episcopate of America
Orthodox Church in America

Dr. Richard L. Hamm

General Minister and President, Christian Church

The passage of scripture that comes back to bless me again and again is Psalm 139.

O Lord, you have searched me and known me.
You know when I sit down and when I rise up;
You discern my thoughts from far away.
You search out my path and lying down,
are aquainted with all my ways.
Even before a word is on my tongue,
O Lord, you know it completely.
You hem me in, behind and before,
and lay your hand upon me.
Such knowledge is too wonderful for me;
it is so high that I cannot attain it.

Where can I go from your spirit?
Or where can I flee from your presence?
If I ascend to heaven, you are there;
if I make my bed in Sheol, you are there.
If I take the wings of the morning
and settle at the farthest limits of the sea,
even there your hand shall lead me,
and your tight hand shall hold me fast.
If I say, "Surely the darkness shall cover me,
and the light around me become night."
even the darkness is not dark to you;
the night is as bright as the day,
for darkness is as light to you.

Psalm 139:1–12

Mary Reath
Publisher

In the middle of working on this book, I heard Ann Mellow, the principal of St. Luke's School in Greenwich Village, read this poem at graduation. I loved it right away because the voice of God is so maternal and mysteriously close, expecially in the line "Don't let yourself lose me."

Gott spricht zu jedem nur, eh er ihn macht

God speaks to each of us as he makes us,
then walks with us silently out of the night.

These are the words we dimly hear:

You, sent out beyond your recall,
go to the limits of your longing.
Embody me.

Flare up like flame
and make big shadows I can move in.

Let everything happen to you: beauty and terror.
Just keep going. No feeling is final.
Don't let yourself lose me.

Nearby is the country they call life.
You will know it by its seriousness.

Give me your hand.

—*Ranier Maria Rilke (1875–1926)*

Scriptural References

Chapter 1 *living*

James B. Hunt, *Luke 11:1-4, New International Version*

Chapter 2 *Loving*

Mangosuthu G. Buthelezi, *Matthew 5:1-12, New International Version*
Art Linkletter, *Mark 10:14-15, New King James Version*

Chapter 3 *Working*

Parris N. Glendening, *Proverbs 29:18, King James Version*
Cesar Pelli, *Ecclesiastes 9:11, King James Version*

Chapter 4 *Doubting*

Desmond Tutu, *Romans 5:1-11, New Oxford Annotated Bible*
Danielle Steel, *Isaiah 41:1, Isaiah 41:13, King James Version*
Al Green, *John 16:33, King James Version*
Robert S. Folkenberg, *John 6:37, King James Version*
Kathleen Norris, *Psalm 27.7 10, The Psalms. Grail Translation from the Hebrew. Chicago. GIA Publications, 1993.*
Don Sundquist, *Psalm 121:1-2, King James Version*
Robert A. Watson, *2 Corinthians 12:9, King James Version*
Dale Evans Rogers, *Hebrews 13:5, King James Version*

photo by Henry Reath

Since 1987, Mary Reath has been the publisher and vice president of Collectors Reprints, Inc., a company that reproduces American classics.

A former elementary school teacher, Reath is the author of God and the Starlight, an anthology of prayers of many faiths for children. She also served as a visiting scholar at the Episcopal Divinity School in Cambridge, Massachusetts.

Reath, her husband, and daughter currently live in Princeton, New Jersey.